# PUZZLES

# PATTERNS

Sarah Khan

QED Publishing

Editorial Director: Victoria Garrard
Art Director: Laura Roberts-Jensen
Designers: Austin Taylor and Rosie Levine
Illustrations by Julie Ingham

First published in the UK in 2014 by
QED Publishing
A Quarto Group company
The Old Brewery
6 Blundell Street
London, N7 9BH

www.qed-publishing.co.uk

A catalogue record for this
book is available from the
British Library.

ISBN 978 1 78171 565 9

Look out for the
puzzles marked as
**Brain Busters** –
they're the hardest!

**Picture credits (fc=front cover,
bc=back cover, t=top, b=bottom,
l=left, r=right)**

**Big Stock:** bctl Home studio
**Shutterstock:** fctl Lightspring, fctr
Ambient Ideas, fct, fccl Bambuh, fctr
Bambuh, fcc etraveler, Yulia Glam, bctc
Nick Kinney, 4 Irina_QQQ, 4 SuslO, 5
Kar, 5tr Aleks Melnik, 6tl Nick Kinney, 6
alexokokok, 6 iana, 10 Neil Leverett, 11
Tribalium, 11b wongstock, 12 gillmar, 14cl
Nick Kinney, 15tr Nick Kinney, 16 , jörg
röse-oberreich, 16t Maria Egupova, 18
SvetlanaR, 19 DVARG, 20t MedusArt, 21tl
fresher, 21t kumnak, 22tr R. Formidable,
22b SuslO, 25 iaRada, 26l JonahWong,
26br freesoulproduction, 27t Fulop Zsolt,
30 De-V, 31 Rodin Anton, 32 Kovalenko
Alexander, 33tc Ikeskinen, 33 LanaN, 33t
VoodooDot, 35tr Nick Kinney, 36 Azuzl,
36t vividvic, 38 Vector, 38 JOAT, 39tr Nick
Kinney, 39t VectorPic, 39 andrewshka,
40 DVARG, 41tr Nick Kinney, 41 Eka
Panova, 42 **007**, 43 Alegria, 43
maximmmmum, 44 MartinaP, 45 LHF
Graphics, 46 RAStudio, 47 Kolesov
Sergei, 47 Undergroundarts.co.uk,
47 Sayid

# Contents

# MISSING SQUARE

Which of the squares below should fill the blank square to complete this pattern?

A

B

C

D

# PATTERN PARTS

Which two of the shapes below aren't part of this pattern?

A

C

E

B

D

F

# LINE SEQUENCE

Which two lines should come next in this sequence?

?

?

# ODD CUSHION OUT

## Which of these cushions is the odd one out?

# BUTTERFLY MATCH

Which one of these butterfly halves doesn't have a matching other half?

# KITE TAIL

Following the sequence, which one of the bows below should complete this kite tail?

A

B

C

D

# STAR SEARCH

There are 9 stars but only 8 star pieces. Which star has no matching piece?

# PATTERN SHAPES

Which of the groups of shapes below can be used to make up this pattern?

# FISH TWINS

Which two of these fish are exactly the same?

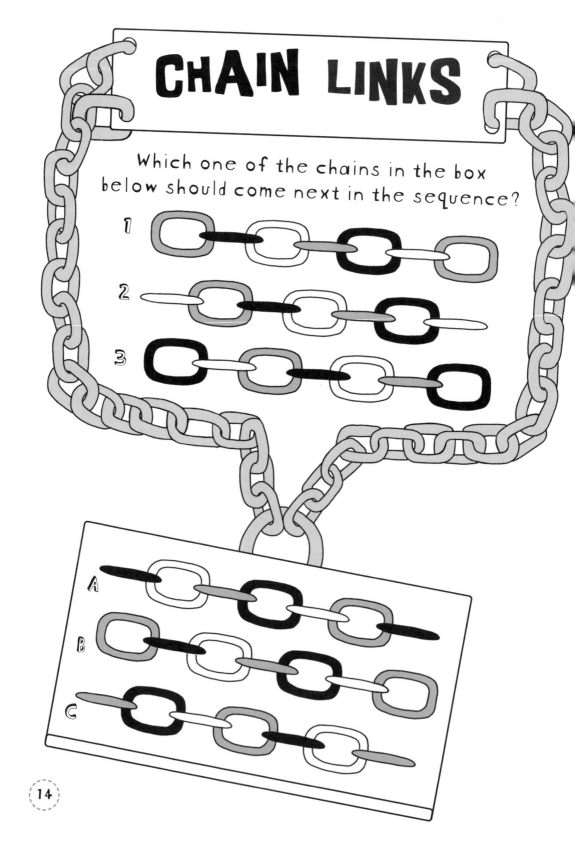

# SPOT THE MISTAKE

BRAIN BUSTER!

In each of these squares, there is a mistake somewhere in the pattern. Can you find it?

A

B

C

D

# PYRAMID PATTERN

Following the pattern, how many stones will pyramid number 10 be made of?

# PATTERN JIGSAW

Which of the jigsaw pieces
below will complete the pattern?

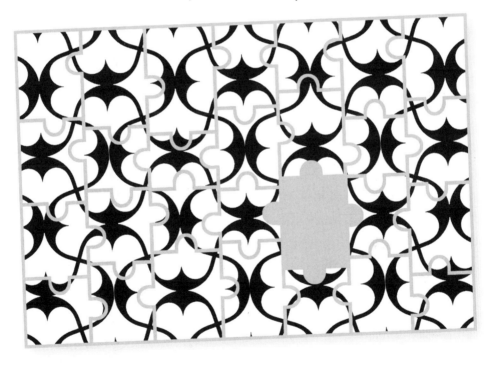

A          B          C

# THE RIGHT ORDER

These pictures show the stages of drawing a pattern, but they are in the wrong order. In what order should they appear?

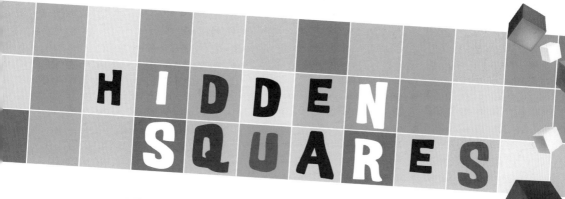

# HIDDEN SQUARES

The pattern on the left is hidden in the block below. Can you find it?

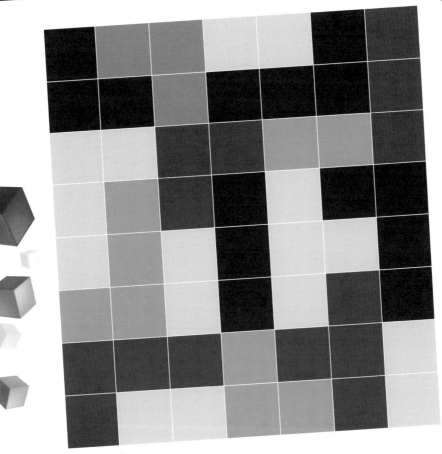

# PATCH-WORK TURTLE

Which three patches on this turtle haven't come from the rolls of material below?

# DOGGY DIFFERENCE

Which one of these dogs is different from the others?

# NUMBER CODE

**BRAIN BUSTER!**

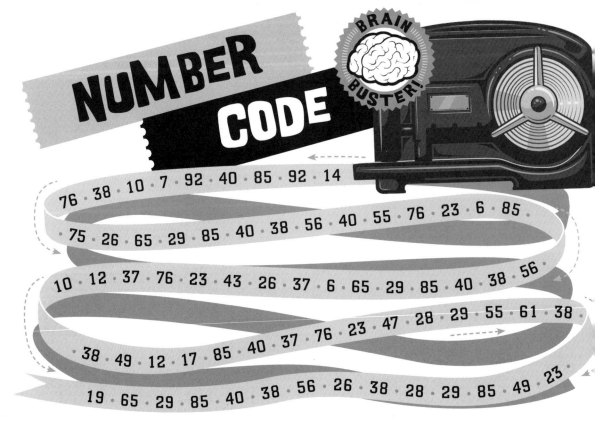

76 · 38 · 10 · 7 · 92 · 40 · 85 · 92 · 14

· 75 · 26 · 65 · 29 · 85 · 40 · 38 · 56 · 40 · 55 · 76 · 23 · 6 · 85 ·

10 · 12 · 37 · 76 · 23 · 43 · 26 · 37 · 6 · 65 · 29 · 85 · 40 · 38 · 56 ·

· 38 · 49 · 12 · 17 · 85 · 40 · 37 · 76 · 23 · 47 · 28 · 29 · 55 · 61 · 38 ·

19 · 65 · 29 · 85 · 40 · 38 · 56 · 26 · 38 · 28 · 29 · 85 · 49 · 23 ·

Secret Agent 770 has received this jumble of numbers from headquarters. In it, he needs to find a pattern of 6 numbers that repeats 3 times.

Find the pattern, decode it using the information on the right, then reorder the letters to discover in which city his mission will be.

A = 14
B = 56
C = 37
D = 7
E = 65
F = 92
G = 6
H = 33

I = 85
J = 76
K = 23
L = 40
M = 49
N = 29
O = 12
P = 82
Q = 55

R = 38
S = 43
T = 28
U = 17
V = 26
W = 75
X = 10
Y = 47
Z = 94

# TREASURE TRAIL

Silverbeard the Pirate has marked three trails on his treasure map. The trail that is made up of a repeating pattern leads to the buried treasure. The other trails are there to confuse anyone who might steal his map. Which trail leads to the treasure?

# ROLLER COASTER

Which of the roller coaster cars below should come next in the sequence?

A    B    C    D

# CATERPILLAR PATTERNS

Following the alphabetical patterns on each caterpillar, which letters should replace the numbers?

# LAUNCH CODE

To launch the rocket, you need to press the correct button on the control panel below. Look carefully at the pattern on the panels of the rocket. Which of the buttons below should come next?

Peppe the pizza chef is a perfectionist. He likes the toppings to be placed in exactly the same place for each type of pizza. There are three types of pizzas below – which one pizza is unlike the other two of its type?

# LEAF PATTERNS

Six leaves have each been split in two. One of the leaves has a symmetrical pattern – one half is the mirror image of the other half. Which are the two halves of this symmetrical leaf?

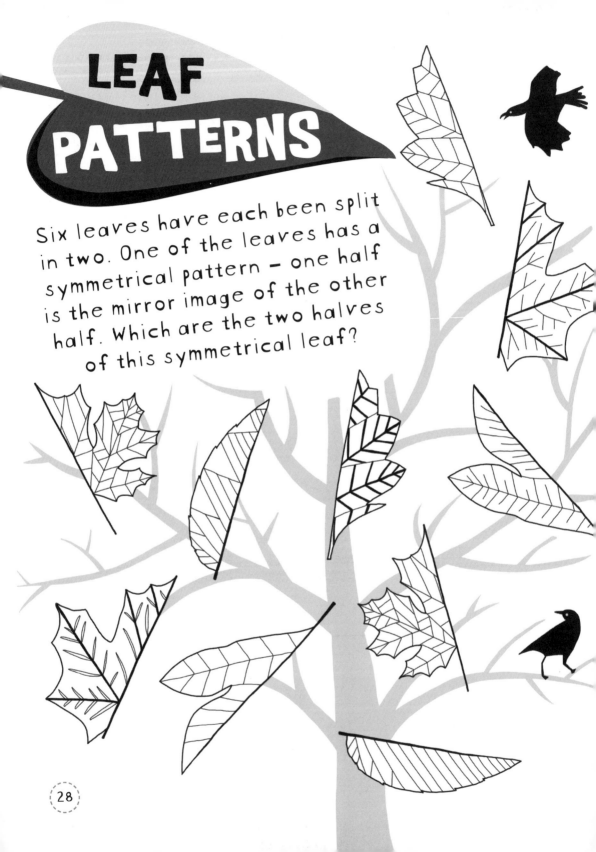

# DOWN THE DRAIN

These bubbles are circling the drain in a repeating pattern. Which three bubbles are out of place?

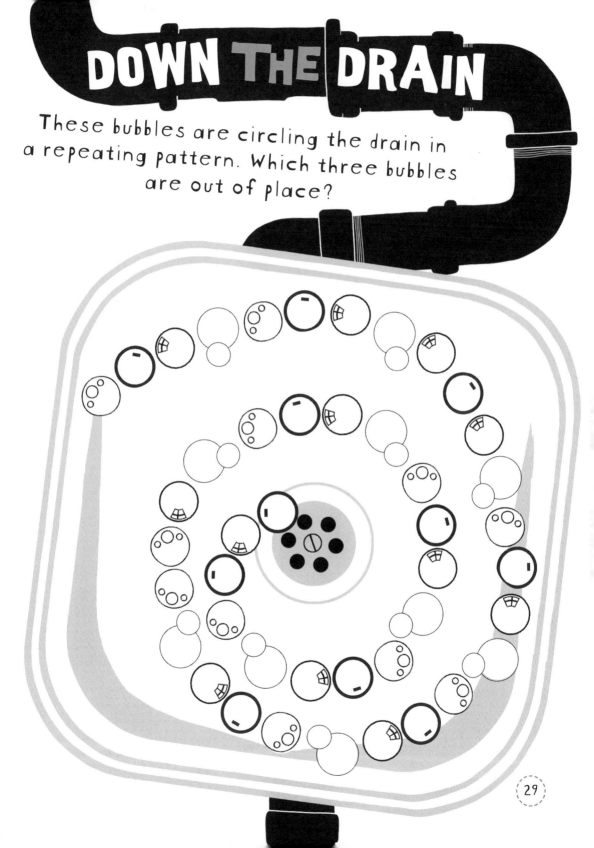

# DOMINOES

Which of the dominoes below should come next in the sequence?

# GRID PATTERN

Find the pattern in the grid. Which of the squares below should replace the blank square?

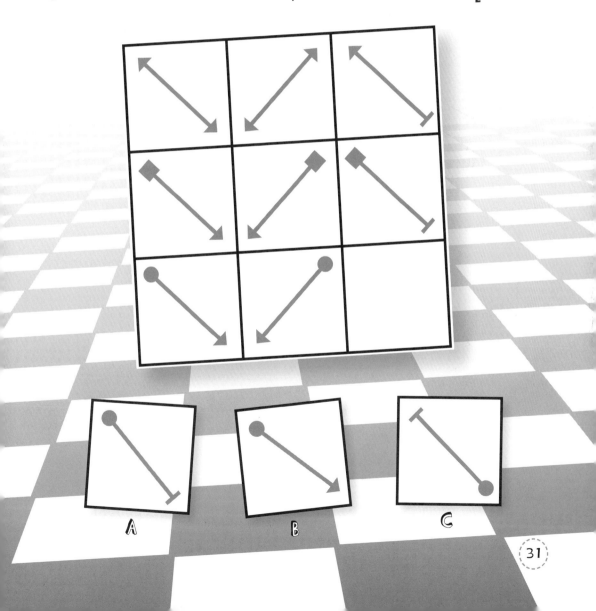

A

B

C

# ODD BUG OUT

Which of these bugs is the odd one out?

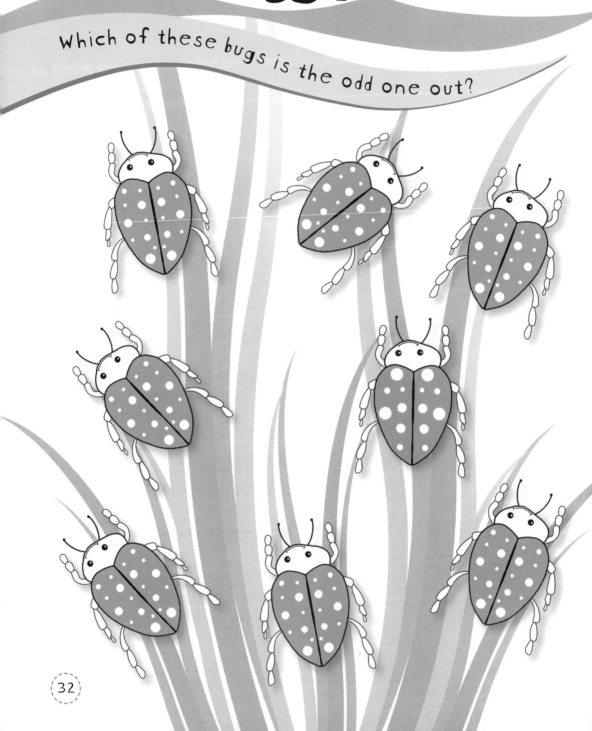

Which of the clocks below
should come next in the sequence?

A

B

C

D

# LIFE CYCLES

Take a look at how the first tadpole changes into a frog. Which of the frogs below will the second tadpole change into?

1

2

A

B

C

# PATCHWORK PATTERN

Find the pattern that links the grids. In Grid **4**, which square should be the snowflake patch?

# POTATO PRINT

Only one of the patterns below could not have been printed using the potato above. Which one?

A

B

C

D

# PYRAMID PUZZLE

There are markings on each stone of this pyramid. The shape of each marking is made by joining together the two shapes on the stones directly beneath it. From the rows below, choose which markings should appear on the numbered stones.

1  ∧ ∨ < >

2  ⌐ ⌐ ⌐ ⌐ ⌐

3  ⊔∨ ⌐∖∖ ⌐∨ ⌐∨

# SALT AND PEPPER

Looking at these salt and pepper shakers, which of the pepper shakers below belongs with the last salt shaker?

A

B

C

# SHIELD SEQUENCE

Which of the shields below should be number **4** in the sequence?

1

2

3

4

A

B

C

# COMPLETE THE CUBE

Which small cube completes the large cube?

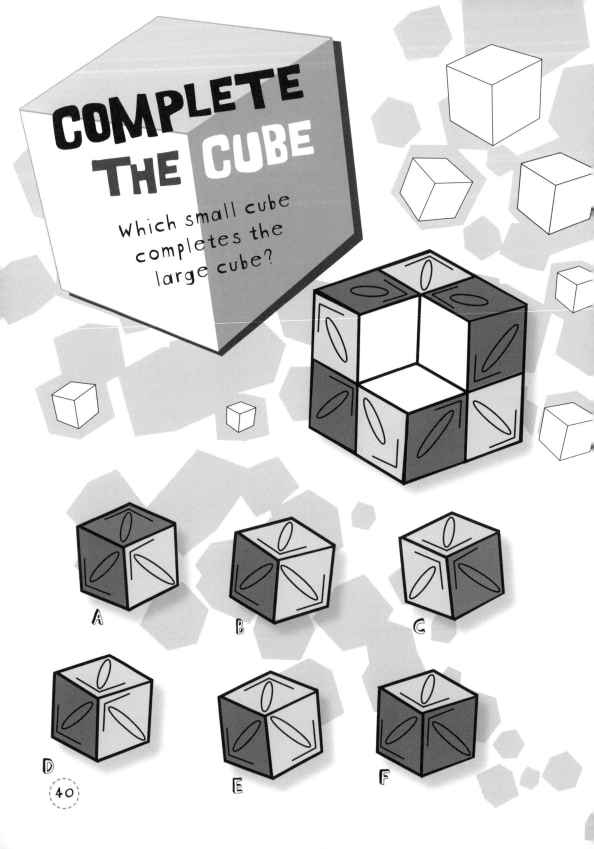

A

B

C

D

E

F

# PATTERN
# MACHINE

BRAIN BUSTER!

The pattern machine takes shapes and makes them into a pattern. Look at the shapes going into and the patterns coming out of the machine. Which of the patterns below should come out of the last machine?

?

A     B     C     D

# PATTERNED PLATES

Following the sequence, what should be the pattern on the last plate on the dinosaur's back?

A     B     C

# SAILING AWAY

Which two of these sailing boats are exactly the same?

A

B

C

D

E

# BIRD COUNT

How many birds are there in the pattern below?

# PASTA PATTERNS

Penny has made these photo frames using pieces of uncooked pasta. Look at the plate of pasta below. Which three types didn't she use?

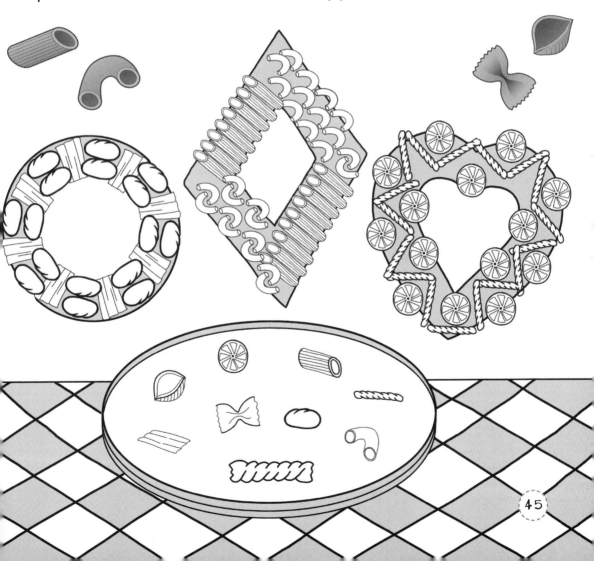

# SEAHORSES

Which two of these seahorses are exactly the same?

# FINGERPRINTS

The police found the fingerprint on the right at a crime scene. It matches one of the fingerprints on their records. Which of the known criminals below was at the crime scene?

TOUGH TERRY

NASTY NATHAN

HORRIBLE HARRY

DODGY DAVE

MEAN MARTY

ROBBING RAY

# Answers

**Page 4**: D
**Page 5**: A and D
**Page 6**:

The pattern is split into three sets of four lines. In each set, the first line from the previous set moves to the bottom.
**Page 7**: C
The black border on the inside shape is missing.
**Page 8**:

**Page 9**: B
**Page 10**: C
**Page 11**:

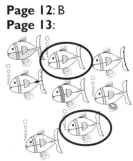

**Page 12**: B
**Page 13**:

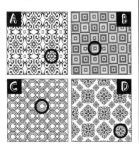

**Page 14**: C
Each stage moves along two links from the previous one and the chain turns on its side.
**Page 15**:

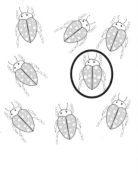

**Page 16**: 66
11+10+9+8+7+6 +5+ 4+ 3+2+1
**Page 17**: C
**Page 18**: 4, 6, 5, 1, 3, 2
**Page 19**:

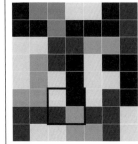

**Page 20**:

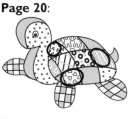

**Page 21**: C
There is an extra patch on his hind leg.
**Page 22**:
65/29/85/40/38/56 = ENILRB = BERLIN
**Page 23**: C
**Page 24**: D
**Page 25**:
1. S - every other letter is missed out.
2. P - the alphabet is backwards and every other letter is missed out.
3. B - every other pair of letters is missed out.
4. Q - the alphabet is backwards and every other pair of letters is missed out.
**Page 26**: B

**Page 27**:

**Page 28**:

**Page 29**:

**Page 30**: B
The dots in the top halves are increasing and the dots in the bottom halves are decreasing.
**Page 31**: A
**Page 32**:

**Page 33**: C
The hour hand is moving forwards by one hour and the minute hand moving forwards by ten minutes.
**Page 34**: B
**Page 35**: F
The top two rows are moving down and the bottom row is moving to the top. Also the order in each row is reversing.
**Page 36**: C
**Page 37**:

**Page 38**: A
**Page 39**: B
The pictures are moving from left to right and changing direction. The marks on the pictures – a triangle, a circle, a rectangle and a line – are moving in a clockwise direction.
**Page 40**: D
**Page 41**: C
**Page 42**: A
**Page 43**: A and D
**Page 44**: 69
**Page 45**:

**Page 46**: C and F
**Page 47**: Mean Marty